# SCOTTISH TARTANS IN FULL COLOR

## James Grant

With an Introduction by
J. Charles Thompson, Fellow of the Scottish Tartans Society

Dover Publications, Inc.
*New York*

Published in Canada by General Publishing Company, Ltd., 30 Lesmill Road, Don Mills, Toronto, Ontario.

Published in the United Kingdom by Constable and Company, Ltd., 3 The Lanchesters, 162–164 Fulham Palace Road, London W6 9ER.

This Dover edition, first published in 1992, contains all 73 color plates from the work originally published under the title *The Tartans of the Clans of Scotland: Also an Introductory Account of Celtic Scotland; Clanship, Chiefs, Their Dress, Arms, Etc., and with Historical Notes of Each Clan*, W. & A. K. Johnston, Edinburgh, 1886. The Introduction by J. Charles Thompson was written specially for the Dover edition. The spelling of many clan names has been adjusted, with subsequent renumbering of the plates.

## DOVER *Pictorial Archive* SERIES

Manufactured in the United States of America
Dover Publications, Inc., 31 East 2nd Street, Mineola, N.Y. 11501

*Library of Congress Cataloging-in-Publication Data*

Grant, James, (1822–1887)
    [Tartans of the clans of Scotland]
    Scottish Tartans in full color / James Grant ; with an introduction by J. Charles Thompson.
        p.     cm.
    Originally published: Tartans of the clans of Scotland. Edinburgh : W. & A. K. Johnston, 1886.
    ISBN 0-486-27046-7 (pbk.)
    1. Tartans—Scotland. 2. Clans—Scotland. I. Title.
DA880.H76G72   1992
929'.2'09411—dc20
                                     91–43221
                                          CIP

# INTRODUCTION

## GRANT'S "TARTAN" BOOK OF 1886

IN 1886 W. & A. K. Johnston of Edinburgh published *The Tartans of the Clans of Scotland* by James Grant, 'author of "The Romance of War," "Old and New Edinburgh," etc.' In spite of its title this book was not really about tartans. Rather it dealt with the clans and their histories, with illustrations of a good many tartans. These were the first printed illustrations of tartans ever published; the earlier books had used illustrations colored by hand or drawn with a complicated contraption of parallel ruling pens. Grant says in his preface that those books "are now rarely to be met with . . . and at greatly enhanced prices." The same is now true, of course, of Grant.

Apparently Johnston's had developed the illustrations and went to a currently popular writer for the text. Grant must have had quite a reputation in his time, but one can just imagine how his title "The Romance of War" would go over today!

There have been many such "tartan" books since, and their titles can be confusingly similar. Grant's was called *The Tartans of the Clans of Scotland*, and a recent one was called *The Tartans of the Scottish Clans*. To keep such similar titles straight, they are usually referred to by author, with dates of those out of print. So the present book is usually called "Grant, 1886."

## THE TEXT

Besides the seventy-three illustrations, Grant's book has three introductory chapters and, with the tartan of each clan, a clan history. A few of the tartans are not related to clans. The Rob Roy tartan and the Prince Charles Edward Stewart are accompanied by romanticized accounts of the respective gentlemen. Grant notes that the Prince Charles Edward tartan, which is first reported in his text, "is nowise different from the Stewart (or Stuart), excepting that the broad red stripe in the latter is very much contracted."

The Hunting Stewart tartan is also first reported in Grant with the following comment, quoted here in its entirety:

> Although we have failed to trace the history of this tartan, or fix the date of its introduction, as it has long been a favourite with the people of Scotland, we thought it right to preserve in this work a record of one of the most beautiful tartans associated with the Royal Stewarts.

All of this material shows a typical Victorian inclination to cite previous authors with little or no attempt to evaluate their statements. Thus the text of Grant's work would be of minimal value as a reprint.

There is no need for an exhaustive review of the introductory chapters or of the historical notes on each clan, but briefly: Chapter I, "Celtic Scotland," divides Highland Scotland at the time of Agricola's invasion (A. D. 81) into "twenty-one aboriginal tribes," from "I. The *Ottadini*" to "XXI. The *Epidii*," with detailed notes on the "topographical position" of each. This information is attributed to "Dr James Browne, whose authorities were the Maps of Ptolemy, and Richard of Cirencester, a monk of the 14th century."

Ptolemy's maps were reasonably contemporary with Agricola's invasion, but he included only a general depiction of North Britain. So all these details must be attributed to a monk, writing more than a thousand years after the event. Yet Grant gives this detailed geography without comment—at third hand. Modern analysis cannot afford to be so uncritical.

Chapter II is titled "Clanship and Chiefs—Dress and Arms." Barely a page of this—a large page, however, in fine print—is on dress and arms, and only four short paragraphs deal with tartan. The whole chapter continues the tendency toward uncritical citation of previous writers, including the remarkable conclusion that the kilt antedates "the great belted plaid of the 16th and 17th centuries." The chronology that is now generally accepted makes the kilt a development from the plaid with the pleats sewn in, so that the top half of the plaid above the belt became a detachable garment.

As for Chapter III, "Some Characteristics of the Highlanders," it perpetuates the romantic view of the "genuine sportsman," loving his "vast stores of legendary poetry" and the bagpipe, that "most ancient musical instrument." His "fidelity to his chief," as a "skilled swordsman" who spoke the "Gaelic . . . language in which there is no word to express *slavery*," is also noted. The "legendary poetry" referred to is that of Ossian, now considered to be at best an eighteenth-century effort inspired by ancient originals and at worst an outright forgery.

The "historical notes" for each clan that follow their respective tartan plates are of the same caliber as the introductory chapters. The first sentence of the note on "The Clan Campbell of Argyll" includes the parenthetical clause, "says a writer," without so much as naming him. The notes merit no more consideration than the introductory chapters, nor would any real purpose be served by reprinting any of them here.

## THE ILLUSTRATIONS

The illustrations are another matter. James D. Scarlett, in *Tartan: The Highland Textile*, calls Grant "the prototype of tartan picture books," and reinforces our judgment of the text, which "has as little to say about tartan as any of them." We have noted that Grant's are the first plates ever printed with a color separation process. At that early date they were not, of course, photo-separation prints. The originals for each color must have been produced by hand. The process used a different ink for each color in the plate (except white). The first impression was a neutral color in a diagonal pattern that could be seen through the other colors to give an accurate suggestion of the diagonal twill weave of tartan. Later colors appear to have been added in order from light to dark.

The results were remarkably good. In a few cases—e. g., Campbell of Breadalbane and Gunn—blacks are not dark enough compared to an adjacent green, but still Grant's process gives a more useful idea of the tartans than a substantial portion of the photographic reproduction in modern tartan texts.

Most of the tartans that Grant gives are taken from *The Authenticated Tartans of the Clans and Families of Scotland*, published in 1850 by the Smith brothers of Mauchline. Their sources were mostly tartan dealers, though they also consulted the noted historian W. F. Skene. A few of Grant's tartans came from Smibert's *The Clans of the Highlands of Scotland*, also from 1850, and from the *Vestiarium Scoticum* or the appendix to Logan's *The Scottish Gael* of 1831, which had measurement charts but no illustrations.

A few of the tartans were original to Grant's book. His MacQuarrie tartan had not been noted before, but strangely enough Grant makes no mention of this fact in his text. The MacLaine of Lochbuie tartan was also previously unpublished, and the original plate number XLIVa indicates that it was added after the other tartans had been collected and numbered. Yet Grant simply notes, without further comment, that "the clans of Lochbuie and Duart were separate, having separate Tartans and Arms." As to the Murray of Tullibardine tartan—also first appearing in his edition—Grant is more informative:

> The Athole [sic] tartan is green, and not unlike that worn by the two battalions of the Black Watch, but with a red stripe through it.
>
> That tartan called the Tullibardine is a red tartan, and was adopted by Charles, first Earl of Dunmore, second son of the first Marquis of Tullibardine, and of Lady Amelia Stanley.

Grant continues with more of the history of Lord Charles Murray and his successors, but adds no more about the tartan.

Any further discussion of each plate is beyond the scope of the present sketch, but a comment or two might be in order. A few of Grant's plates—as might be expected in a work of that magnitude—include errors. MacLaren and MacNaughton show slight differences between the horizontal and vertical pattern. A few others differ slightly from earlier versions that are now preferred, but none of these is of importance except to scholars of tartan.

A few of Grant's tartans have fallen out of use. His Drummond is little used compared to another pattern called Drummond of Perth. The Sutherland plate shows the Black Watch tartan. That tartan was also worn by the Argyll and Sutherland Highlanders, and many of them wore it home. It is still considered an alternate Sutherland tartan, but the one shown in most modern books has two white stripes and a triple red added to the Black Watch. Several other tartans, civilian and military—Gordon, Murray of Atholl, MacKenzie, Lamont, Forbes and Campbell of Argyll—were formed in the same way, by adding light stripes to the Black Watch, which was the original military tartan.

The plates vary widely in scale. Some show several repeats of the sett (the whole pattern of the tartan), while others do not show enough to be sure of just what the pattern is, particularly Cameron of Lochiel and MacDougall. The Ross plate not only does not reveal a full repeat, it fails to show correctly the part of the sett it covers. The Ogilvie plate does show a full repeat, but not enough more to be sure without comparing it with other sources. The sett—so much more complex than any of the others—suggests that the original sample may have been woven in silk.

## THE GREAT TARTAN MYTH

Since Grant says so little about tartan, it will be worth our while to include a brief sketch of tartan and its history.

Tartan can be defined as cloth woven from wool of different colors in a checkered pattern, and a piece of fabric of this description, woven from natural light and dark wools, has been found in a cache with coins dating from the Roman presence in Britain. A passage from the first century B.C. (Virgil, *Aeneid*, Book VIII, line 660) is universally accepted as the first reference to tartan. It reads: *virgatis lucent sagulis,* "they [the Celts] shine with striped cloaks."*

But the Great Tartan Myth held that the different setts for each clan were as old as the *Aeneid,* and this myth was widely accepted in Grant's time. In point of fact it seems likely that until about 1800 each time the weaver wound a warp he created a new pattern. In early portraits showing two garments on the same person there will be two different tartans. The only common exception would be a jacket and trews,

which would be a suit cut from a single length of cloth. A portrait of two MacDonald boys, which can be seen at Armadale Castle, shows five different tartans between the two of them, none of the five being just like any sett in use today as a MacDonald tartan.

The only pattern commonly seen repeated in early portraits is a plain red-and-black check. It is usually called MacGregor (Rob Roy)—though Grant simply calls it Rob Roy—because portraits of that gentleman show him wearing it. The same pattern is also seen, however, in portraits of other gentlemen who had no connection with the Clan Gregor. Presumably the weaver in each case had a supply of wool in the two colors and was not overburdened with imagination.

There are two illuminating incidents from Bonnie Prince Charlie's attempt in 1745 to reconquer the throne of Britain for his father who remained in France. The father was known as the Old Pretender and would have been James VIII of Scotland and III of Britain. Both of these incidents involved a confusion as to clan membership, and in neither instance was any attention paid to the tartan.

In the first case two units of MacDonalds met. One group was Jacobite—for James (*Jacobus* is the Latin for James)—and the other was made up of the opposing Hanoverians. The author who described the confusion that resulted said they were all clearly MacDonalds; they were all wearing heather in their bonnets. The only distinguishing features were the black cockades of the Hanoverians and the white ones of the Jacobites.

The other incident occurred after the final Jacobite disaster at Culloden in 1746. The victorious Hanoverians were going over the battlefield bayoneting their wounded enemies when one of the latter cried, "Haud your hand! I'm a Campbell." The Campbells had been Hanoverians, and the assailants excused their mistake by pointing out that the man had lost his bonnet.

"Somebody hath struck it off my head," was the reply. It is not recorded whether the missing mark of identification was the black cockade or the sprig of bog myrtle that would have marked him as a Campbell. The point is, though, that in the mid-eighteenth century, in cases when clan identification became a problem, no mention is made of MacDonald or Campbell tartans. This is particularly striking in the second case, where the man must have been wearing tartan, or they wouldn't have been finishing him off. Even in the unlikely event that he might have been dressed in hodden grey, they didn't ask about tartan, but only about his missing bonnet.

More evidence on this subject is found in a pattern book issued in 1819 by Wilson's of Bannockburn, the leading tartan weaver of the day. It showed some 250 different setts, but only about a third of them had names. There were clan names, family names and a few named for cities. Being 1819, there was a Wellington tartan and a Waterloo tartan. There was also a Coburg tartan; Queen Victoria's mother was a Coburg. But most of the setts had only a number to identify them.

Only about a third of Wilson's named setts still use today the names they went under in 1819. Most of the rest have simply been forgotten, though a few of those named for towns—Aberdeen and Dundee, for example—have been revived in the last couple of decades. Of greatest interest to this discussion are the setts now known by different names from the ones they had in 1819. Wilson's Coburg is now Graham of Menteith, and his New Bruce is now called MacColl. Clearly the naming of tartans was just getting started in 1819.

We must accept, then, that although tartan itself is of great antiquity, different setts for the identification of clans cannot go much further back than 1800. How, then, did the myth of the antiquity of clan tartans ever originate? We can only conjecture.

First we must remember the time frame—the height of the Romantic Revival, which affected all of Europe and spread into art and music as well as literature. Its leader in Scotland was Sir Walter Scott, whose Waverly novels were the rage throughout the English-speaking world. But, of course, Sir Walter's Highlands were no closer to any reality than Zane Grey's Wild West.

Just who first suggested an ancient system of clan tartans can

---

*This passage has been universally misquoted and mistranslated in books on tartan. Virgil's *sagulis* has been erroneously given as *sagalis.* It is not certain who first made this mistake but later writers copied it, apparently without exception. The translation offered has been as universally erroneous. *Sagulis* is taken as the subject, which is impossible, since it is in the ablative case. The subject is *Galli,* in line 657, and the correct translation is as we give it. Remember the Romans called the Celts "Gauls." The first sentence of Caesar's *Gallic Wars* begins, "All Gaul is divided into three parts," and ends, "those who in their own language are called *Celtae,* in ours *Galli.*"

probably never be determined. When realists asked what had happened to the system, they were told, "Why, the tartan was proscribed after Culloden, so all the old clan tartans were forgotten." If anyone pointed out that the proscription only lasted thirty-eight years—hardly long enough for a long-cherished system to have faded from memory—they were ignored. There was nothing people wanted more than an ancient clan tartan system, and they were determined to have one.

Someone will always turn up to supply an urgent demand, and two most remarkable characters appeared at this juncture. They were said to be two long-lost grandsons of Bonnie Prince Charlie. They never made this claim themselves, but they did not protest when their friends proposed it.

People objected, "Don't be foolish; the Prince never had any lawful issue."

"But he did," they replied. "When Princess Louisa retired to that convent, it wasn't to escape Prince Charlie's neglect and mistreatment. She was going to have a baby, and she knew the Hanovers would have it destroyed"—a not illogical assumption under the circumstances—"and that baby was adopted by Admiral Allen." Their father had indeed been adopted, the dates were about right, and nobody ever proved they were not actually the Prince's grandsons. There was, in fact, a striking physical resemblance between the elder of them and the late Prince. The two started as John and Charles Allen, but Princess Louisa had been a Sobieska, and they were eventually known as the Sobieski Stuarts.

Nobody seems to have taken note of the fact that the Princess was still alive—living in a palazzo on the Lung'Arno in Florence.

Their next claim was that they had discovered a sixteenth-century manuscript describing some seventy-two clan tartans. They never produced the original—their father, they said, had it in London and was annoyed that they had so much as mentioned having it. All anyone ever saw was a "corrupt copy" with "1721" scribbled on the first page. It is known as the Cromarty MS.

This may have had something to do with the visit of George IV to Scotland in 1824, stage-managed by Sir Walter Scott. The King let it be known that he would appear at a levee at Holyrood House, wearing a kilt of Royal Stuart tartan. All of the lords and chiefs were expected to appear in their respective tartans as well, and apparently some of them went to the two Sobieskis for advice. In any case, word of the Cromarty MS began to be circulated about this time.

The brothers did not publish until 1842. The book was called *Vestiarium Scoticum*, which is Latin for "The Scottish Wardrobe," and it became the subject of immediate and heated controversy. Sir Walter Scott called the MS "utterly false, a most feeble and clumsy imitation," and the first chemist who examined it said it had "been treated with chemical agents in order to give the writing a more aged appearance."

But the proponents were many. They took the MS to a second chemist who opined that he "could not say that it was not an old MS." Besides, Sir Walter's doubts had been expressed privately, and everybody wanted the *Vestiarium* tartans, though over fifty of them had never been heard of before. It has since been proved (see Bibliography 5, below) that the *Vestiarium* was a forgery, but this should not be given too much weight. Every tartan sett was invented sometime by somebody, and the original claim that these were older than they proved to be doesn't matter so much now. After all, they are a century and a half old, and only a handful of named tartans are older.

The invention of tartans has proceeded apace. Over 2,000 setts have been listed. The *Vestiarium* gave setts for Lowland houses as well as Highland clans—another thing Sir Walter took exception to—and many families within the clans have their own setts to add to the clan tartans. The provinces of Canada have each an official tartan, and states in the U.S. are following suit. The Royal Canadian Air Force has an official tartan and U.S. forces are designing them, officially or otherwise. The clans and families are branching out with Dress and Hunting tartans, and the same sett—any sett—may be produced in dark "modern," lighter "ancient" or "muted" color schemes. Actually anybody can design a sett, name it—or not if they don't care to—and have it woven if they can afford it. In the absence of any real control, it would take a long book to disentangle the confusion.

There have been dozens of "tartan" books, too, but most of them are clan books or history books with some tartan illustrations. In fact there have been so few books truly devoted to tartan that it is worth listing them in a bibliography with a brief comment on each.

## BIBLIOGRAPHY

1. Sobieski Stuart, J. S. S. and C. E. *Vestiarium Scoticum*, 1842, William Taft, Edinburgh. Discussed above, and in 5, below.

2. Stewart, D. W. *Old and Rare Scottish Tartans*, 1893, Geo. P. Johnston, Edinburgh. A selection of interesting setts in a small enough edition for the illustrations to be tipped-in pieces of woven silk, perhaps the best method—and certainly one of the most original—ever devised for tartan illustration.

3. Stewart, Donald C. *The Setts of the Scottish Tartans*, 1950, Oliver & Boyd, Edinburgh. A weaver's book with thread-counts of 261 tartans and historical notes on the origins of each sett. The late D. C. Stewart was deservedly known as "the father of modern tartan research." He was the son of D. W. Stewart (see 2, above), and *The Setts* was his magnum opus.

4. Scarlett, James D. *The Tartans of the Scottish Clans*, 1975, Wm. Collins Sons, Glasgow and London. This was a reprint of an earlier "tartan" book that was really a clan book like Grant, 1886—note the similarity of the titles! The crucial difference is that Scarlett added a paragraph or two about the source and history of each of the tartans. This book is unfortunately now out of print.

Scarlett inherited all of D. C. Stewart's tartan papers and could probably claim—as D. C. could have in his time—to know more about the tartan than any other man alive. He has written several other books that would be included here if space permitted and one that cannot be passed over (see 6, below).

5. Stewart, Donald C., and Thompson, J. Charles. *Scotland's Forged Tartans*, 1980, Paul Harris, Edinburgh. This was an exposé of the *Vestiarium Scoticum*. Thompson had obtained photographs of the Cromarty MS, the "corrupt copy" that the brothers had circulated before they published, allegedly from the genuine MS that no one had ever seen. He transcribed the MS and his transcription is given between Stewart's substantive proofs of the *Vestiarium's* falsity and his own linguistic analysis. Sir Walter Scott had said from the first the document was "false . . . feeble and clumsy," but he simply stated that as his opinion. Thompson proves it by citing a host of examples and then goes on to show, through examples of partial corrections made between the MS and the published version, that the Sobieskis knew the MS was false.

Stewart never got this paper published, and it was among the literary effects inherited by Scarlett, who wrote an introduction, added a transcription of the Lauder MS (a contemporary copy of the Cromarty MS) and found a publisher.

6. Scarlett, James D. *Tartan: The Highland Textile*, 1990, Shepheard-Walwyn, London. This book reprints the thread-counts and relevant commentary from Stewart's *Setts* (see 3, above). It adds to Stewart's remarks on each sett wherever new material is available and adds 201 thread-counts for a total of 462. Before starting with the thread-counts, however, "Part One: Textile and Art Form" covers history, weaving and research. This is now the final word on the tartan and likely to remain so for a good, long time.

J. CHARLES THOMPSON
*Fellow of the Scottish Tartans Society*

# LIST OF TARTANS

PLATE 1. Buchanan.

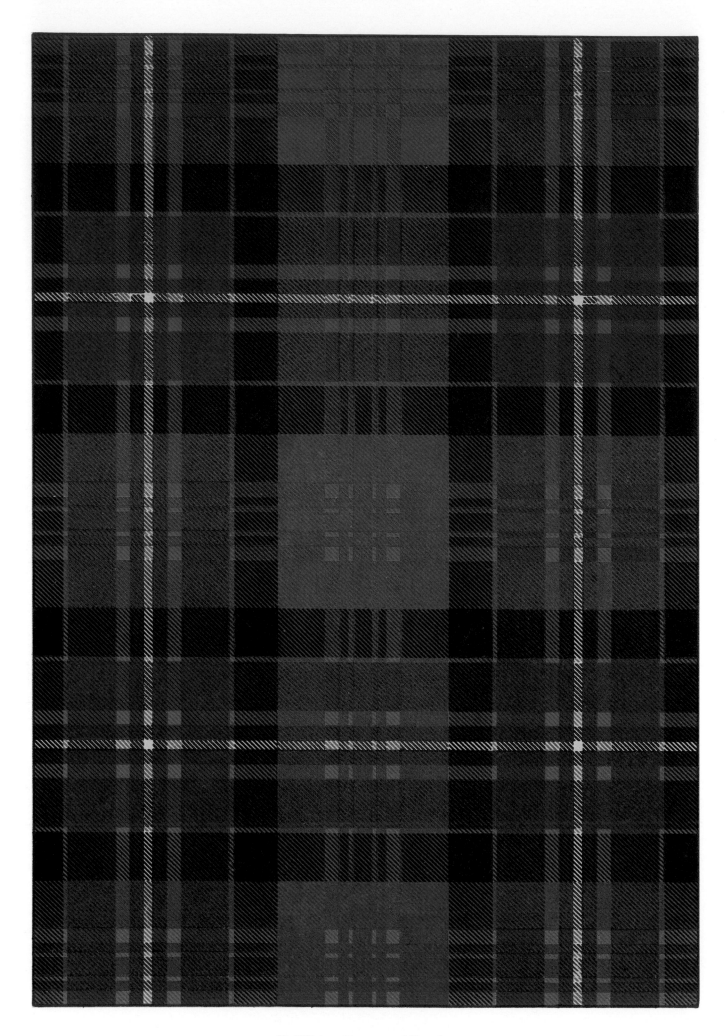

PLATE 2.    Cameron of Erracht.

PLATE 3.    Cameron of Lochiel.

PLATE 4.    Campbell of Argyll.

PLATE 5. Campbell of Breadalbane.

PLATE 6. Campbell of Cawdor.

PLATE 7. Campbell of Loudoun.

PLATE 8.    Chisholm.

PLATE 9. Clergy.

PLATE 10.    Colquhoun.

PLATE 11. Cumin.

PLATE 12.  Drummond.

PLATE 13.    Farquharson.

PLATE 14.  Fergusson.

PLATE 15.  Forbes.

PLATE 16. Fraser.

PLATE 17.   Gordon.

PLATE 18. Graham.

PLATE 19.   Grant.

PLATE 20.   Gunn.

PLATE 21. Jacobite.

PLATE 22.    Lamont.

PLATE 23. Leslie.

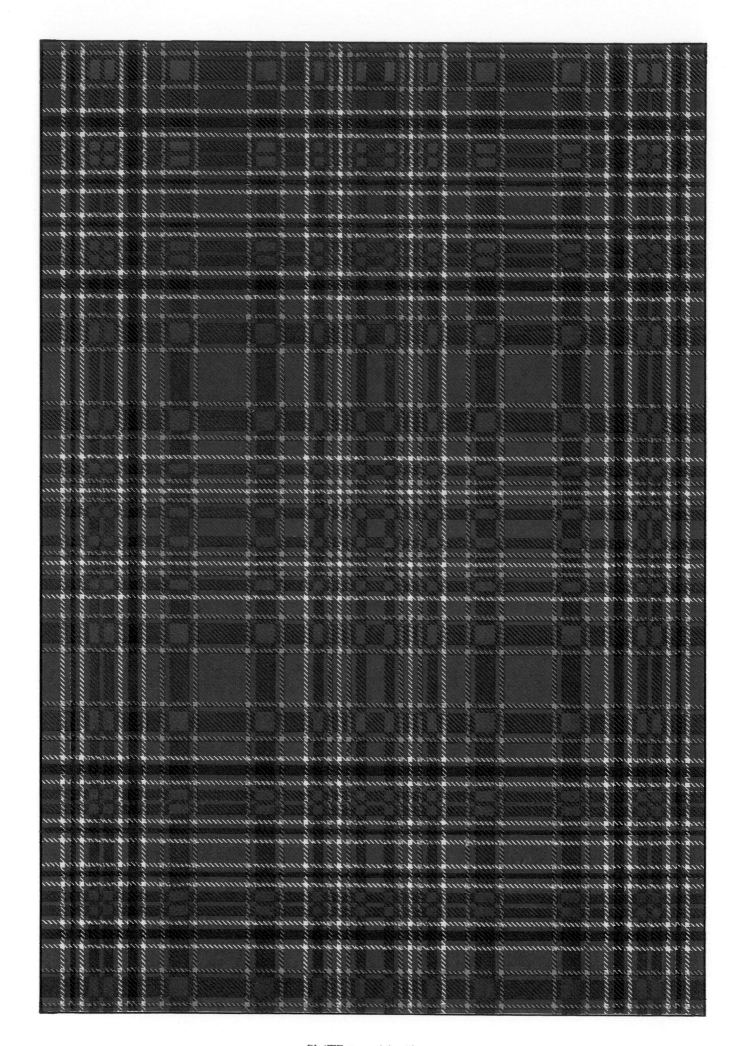

PLATE 24. MacAlister.

PLATE 25. MacAulay.

PLATE 26.   MacDonald.

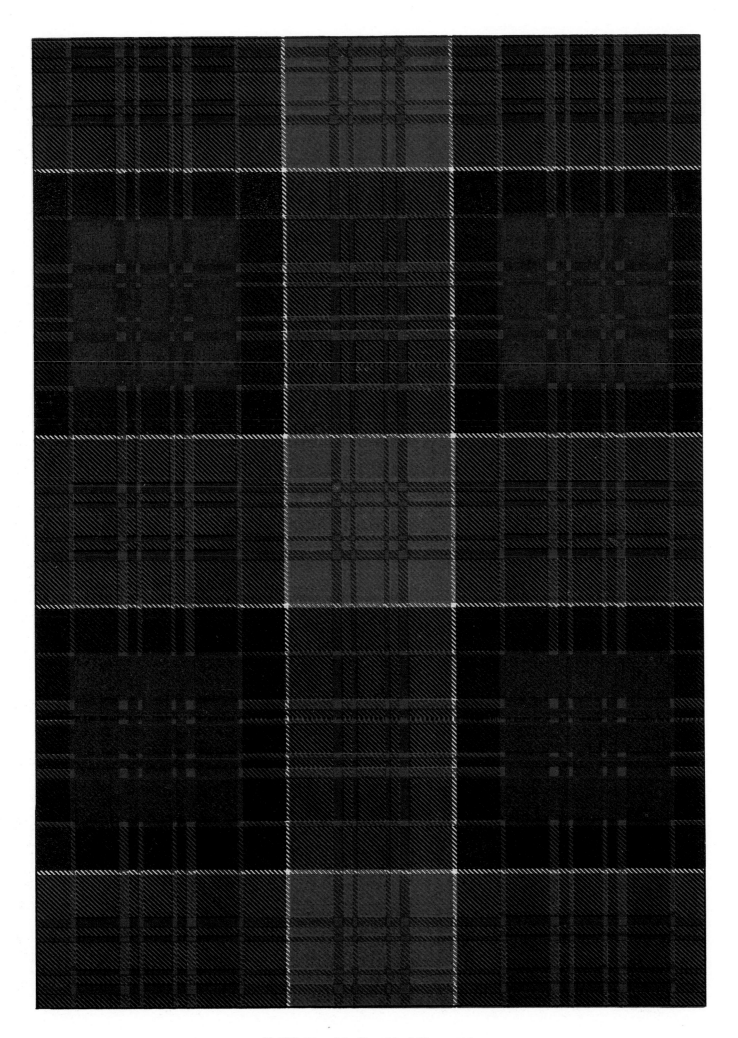

PLATE 27. MacDonald of Clanranald.

PLATE 28. MacDonald of Glengarry.

PLATE 29.   MacDonald of the Isles.

PLATE 30.    MacDonald of Staffa.

PLATE 31. MacDougall.

PLATE 32. MacDuff.

PLATE 33. MacFarlane.

PLATE 34.   MacGillivray.

PLATE 35. MacGregor.

PLATE 36. Macintyre.

PLATE 37. Mackay.

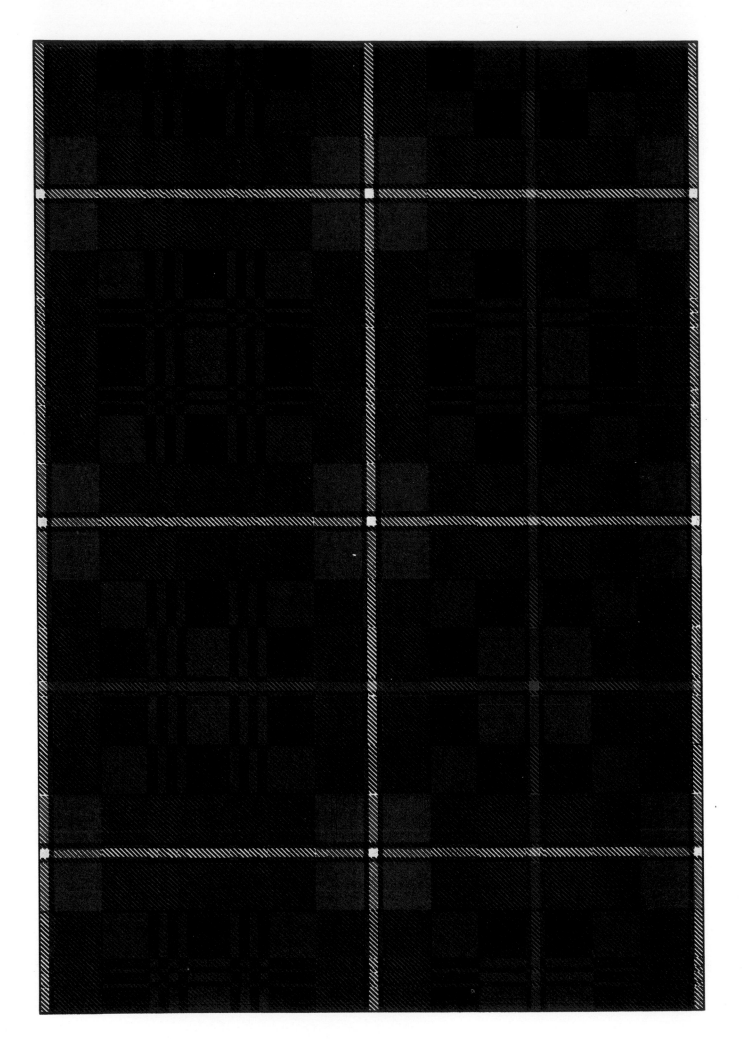

PLATE 38. MacKenzie.

PLATE 39.   MacKinnon.

PLATE 40.    Mackintosh.

PLATE 41.   Mackintosh, Chief.

PLATE 42. MacLachlan.

PLATE 43.   MacLaine of Lochbuie.

PLATE 44. MacLaren.

PLATE 45. MacLean of Duart.

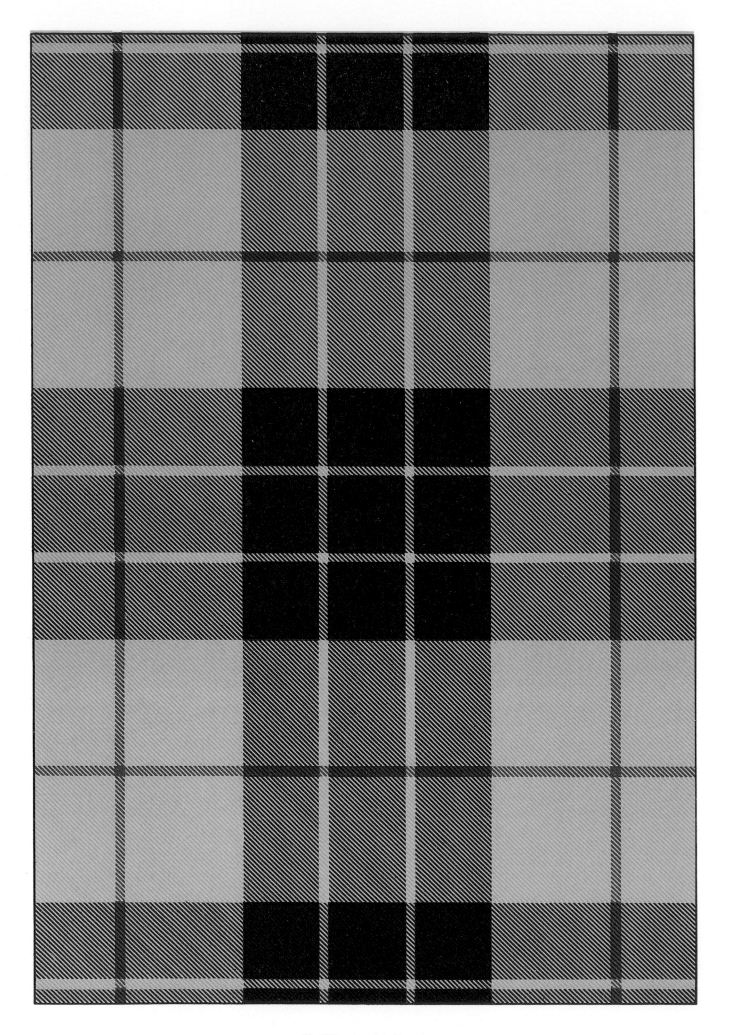

PLATE 46.  MacLeod.

PLATE 47.   Macnab.

PLATE 48.   MacNaughton.

PLATE 49. MacNeil.

PLATE 50. MacPherson.

PLATE 51. MacPherson, Hunting.

PLATE 52. MacQuarrie.

PLATE 53.   MacRae.

PLATE 54. Malcolm.

PLATE 55. Matheson.

PLATE 56. Menzies.

PLATE 57. Munro.

PLATE 58.  Murray of Atholl.

PLATE 59.  Murray of Tullibardine.

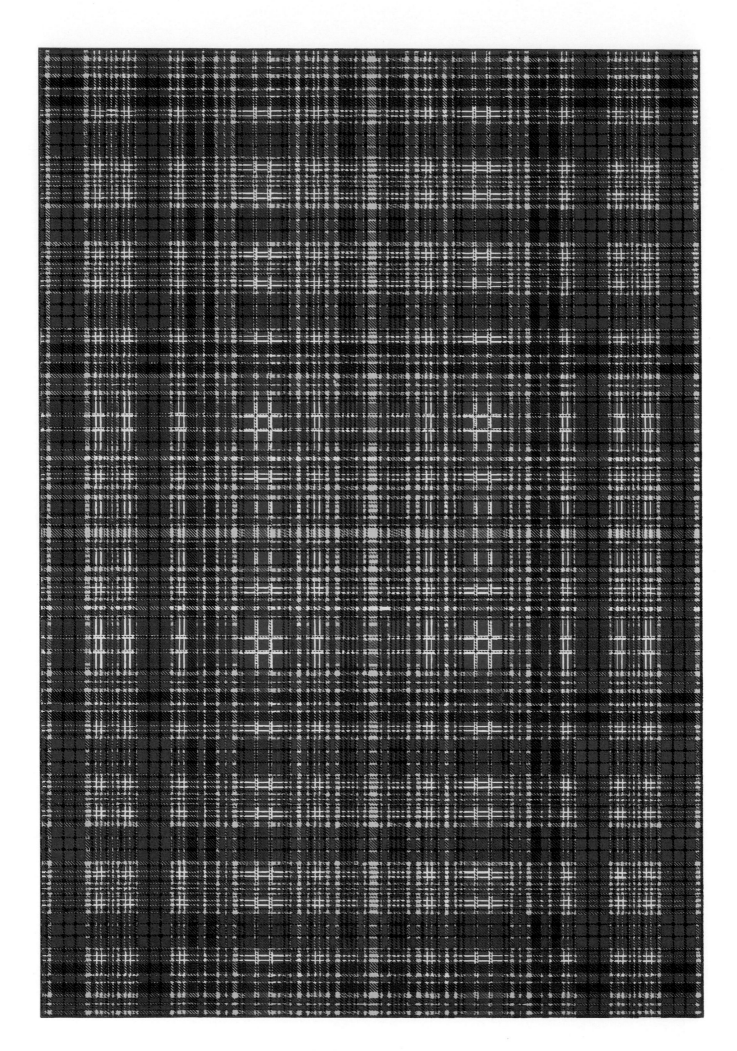

PLATE 60. Ogilvie.

PLATE 61. Rob Roy.

PLATE 62.   Robertson.

PLATE 63.  Ross.

PLATE 64. Sinclair.

PLATE 65.  Skene.

PLATE 66. Stewart, Hunting.

PLATE 67.   Stewart, Old.

PLATE 68.    Stewart, Prince Charles Edward.

PLATE 69.    Stewart, Royal.

PLATE 70.   Stewart, Dress.

PLATE 71.   Sutherland.

PLATE 72. Urquhart.

PLATE 73.   The Duke of Rothesay in Highland Costume.